North
Sea

WADDEN SEA

GRONINGEN

FRIESLAND

DRENTHE

NORTH
HOLLAND

IJSSELMEER

OVERIJSSEL

NETHERLANDS

☆

AMSTERDAM

THE HAGUE

UTRECT

SOUTH
HOLLAND

UTRECT

GELDERLAND

ROTTERDAM

NORTH BRABANT

GER

ZEELAND

LIMBURG

BELGIUM

A BLOOM OF FRIENDSHIP

The Story of the Canadian Tulip Festival

WRITTEN BY
Anne Renaud

ILLUSTRATED BY
Ashley Spires

Lobster Press™

A Bloom of Friendship: The Story of the Canadian Tulip Festival
Text © 2004 Anne Renaud
Illustrations © 2004 Ashley Spires
Map Illustrations: Malcolm Cullen

Published by Lobster Press™
1620 Sherbrooke Street West, Suites C & D
Montréal, Québec H3H 1C9
Tel. (514) 904-1100 • Fax (514) 904-1101
www.lobsterpress.com

Publisher: Alison Fripp
Editors: Alison Fripp & Karen Li
Book Designer: Lynda Arthur
Production Manager: Tammy Desnoyers

We acknowledge the financial support of the Government of Canada through the Book Publishing Industry Development Program (BPIDP) for our publishing activities.

The Canada Council | Le Conseil des Arts
for the Arts | du Canada

We acknowledge the support of the Canada Council for the Arts for our publishing program.

National Library of Canada Cataloguing in Publication

Renaud, Anne, 1957-
     A bloom of friendship : the story of the Canadian Tulip Festival / Anne Renaud ; illustrated by Ashley Spires.

(My Canada)
Includes bibliographical references.
ISBN 1-894222-89-X

     1. Canadian Tulip Festival--History--Juvenile literature. 2. Flower festivals--Ontario--Ottawa--Juvenile literature. I. Spires, Ashley, 1978- II. Title. III. Series.

GT4813.A4O77 2004   j394.26971384   C2004-901990-2

Printed and bound in India.

Dedicated to my uncle Thomas Delaney who, alongside thousands of other brave souls, fought to restore light and freedom in a time of obscurity and oppression.
– Anne

To Mom and Dad, Thank You.
– Ashley

The author would like to extend her heartfelt gratitude to the following people who generously provided their knowledge, memories, photographs, artifacts and general support for this book. To Desmond Morton, professor of history at McGill University and author of A Military History of Canada, and Andrew Burtch, researcher at the Canadian War Museum, for their help with the military passages of the manuscript. To Thomas Delaney, Frank V. Stanton, and Helena Howes for imparting their experiences of war. To Barbara Karsh and Tess Taconis for sharing the visually eloquent work of their husbands, Malak Karsh and Kryn Taconis. To Doug Little of the Ottawa Tulip Festival; Hariette Fried and Serge Blondin of the City of Ottawa Archives; Carol Cowan of the Netherlands Flower Bulb Information Centre; Dorota Grudniewicz, landscape architect with the National Capital Commission; Nava Silvera of Yad Vashem in Jerusalem; and Charles Welling of the Atlas Van Stolk in Rotterdam. To the staff at the Canadian War Museum; the National Library of Canada; the National Archives of Canada; the Montreal Holocaust Memorial Centre; and the Westmount Library. Finally, to my editor at Lobster Press, Karen Li, whose guidance, patience, indulgence, and overall good nature have made the publication of my first book a memorable experience.

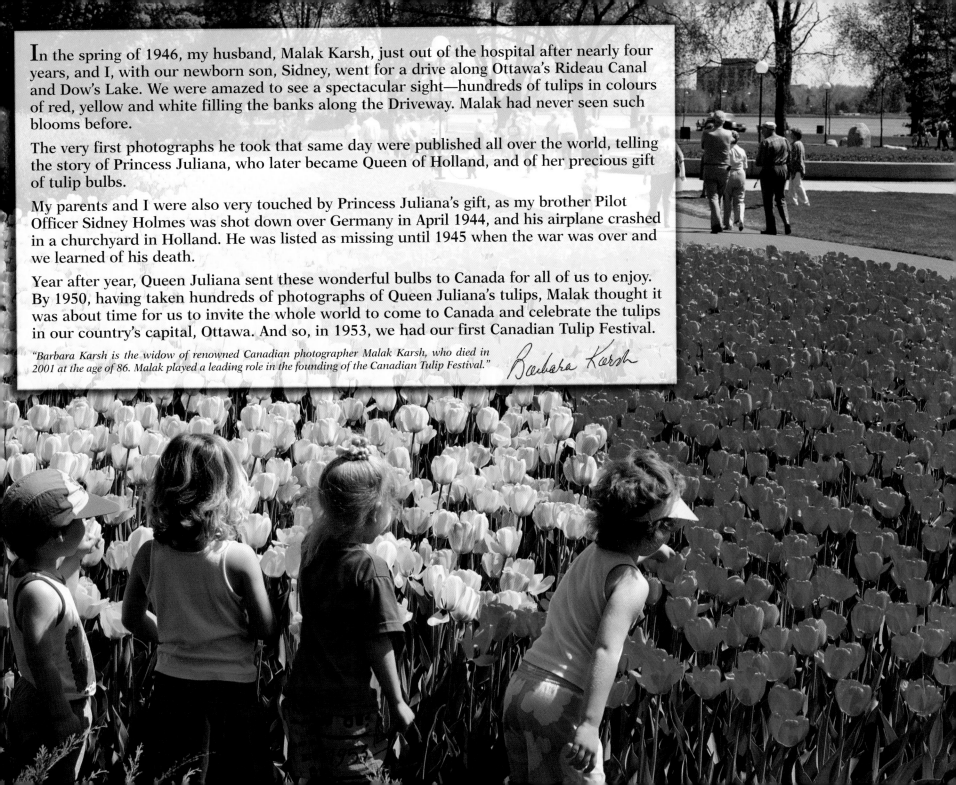

In the spring of 1946, my husband, Malak Karsh, just out of the hospital after nearly four years, and I, with our newborn son, Sidney, went for a drive along Ottawa's Rideau Canal and Dow's Lake. We were amazed to see a spectacular sight—hundreds of tulips in colours of red, yellow and white filling the banks along the Driveway. Malak had never seen such blooms before.

The very first photographs he took that same day were published all over the world, telling the story of Princess Juliana, who later became Queen of Holland, and of her precious gift of tulip bulbs.

My parents and I were also very touched by Princess Juliana's gift, as my brother Pilot Officer Sidney Holmes was shot down over Germany in April 1944, and his airplane crashed in a churchyard in Holland. He was listed as missing until 1945 when the war was over and we learned of his death.

Year after year, Queen Juliana sent these wonderful bulbs to Canada for all of us to enjoy. By 1950, having taken hundreds of photographs of Queen Juliana's tulips, Malak thought it was about time for us to invite the whole world to come to Canada and celebrate the tulips in our country's capital, Ottawa. And so, in 1953, we had our first Canadian Tulip Festival.

"Barbara Karsh is the widow of renowned Canadian photographer Malak Karsh, who died in 2001 at the age of 86. Malak played a leading role in the founding of the Canadian Tulip Festival."

Barbara Karsh

A Blanket of Tulips

Every spring, Canada's capital bursts into colour with thousands of tulip blooms.

Although this annual event has much to do with a love of flowers, it is, above all, the celebration of a friendship that blossomed between two countries more than half a century ago.

This is one of the many stories of the dark days of the Second World War.

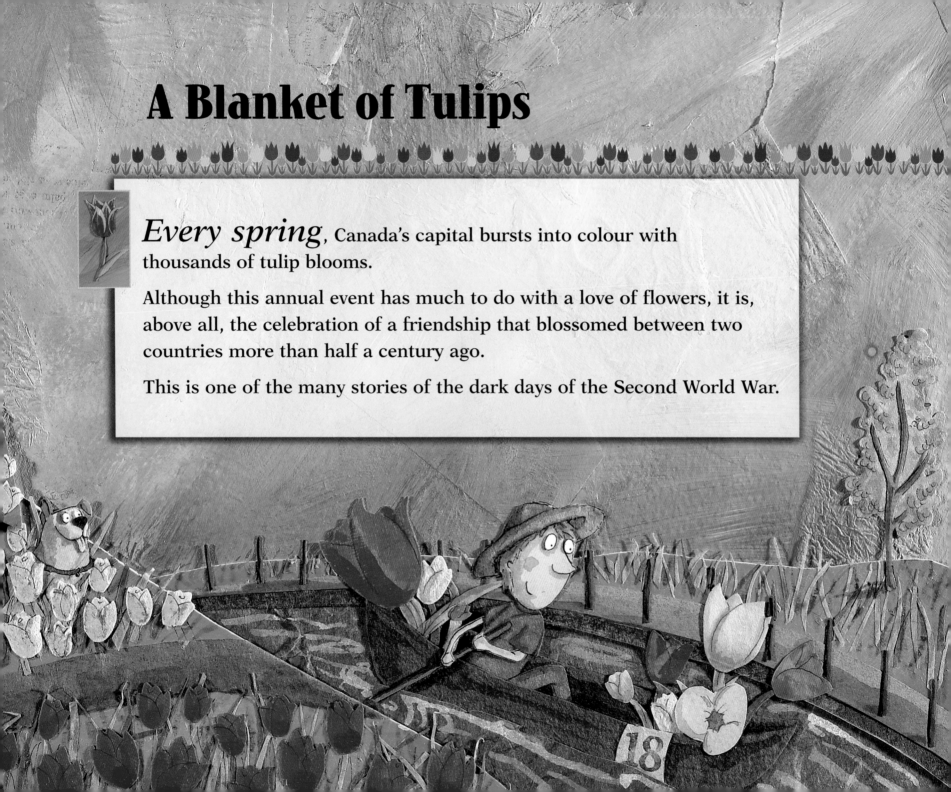

Hitler's Germany

The Gazette.

WEATHER FORECAST:
Partly cloudy and cool;
possibly light showers.
For complete weather reports see Page Nine.

Temperature Yesterday
Max.: 68; Min.: 53
Same Date Last Year
Max.: 63; Min.: 44

VOL. CLXVIII. No. 217

MONTREAL, MONDAY SEPTEMBER 11, 1939.—TWENTY-FOUR PAGES

PRICE FIVE CENT

Canada Declares War by House Decision; Lapointe Proclaims Loyalty of Quebec; French Troops Mass On Italian Border

Courtesy of the Montreal Gazette

In the 1930s a new government called the National Socialist German Workers' Party came to power in Germany. These new leaders were also known as the Nazis. Holding to extremely racist beliefs and the conviction that Germany was destined to rule the world, Adolf Hitler, the leader of the Nazis, set out to conquer the rest of Europe. 🌷

On September 1, 1939, German tanks rolled into Poland.

Within days, France and Britain, who had promised to support Poland in case of an attack, declared war on Germany. On the other side of the Atlantic, Canada, a partner in the **Commonwealth**, decided to follow in Britain's footsteps. On Sunday, September 10, 1939, Prime Minister William Lyon MacKenzie King announced that Canadians would fight against Germany. The following morning, newspaper headlines shouted the news: Canada was at war! 🌷

Swastika 🌷

Instant History Facts

🌷 Hitler believed that all people were of "superior" or "inferior" blood and that German blood was the greatest of all. He also believed that it was necessary to keep the German blood "pure" by eliminating all "inferiors." Those considered to be "inferior" included the physically and mentally challenged, criminals, old people, homosexuals, Gypsies, Russians, Poles and, in particular, Jewish people.

🌷 The **Commonwealth** is a group of countries, including Canada and Great Britain, that acknowledges the Queen of England as their symbolic ruler.

🌷 For many cultures, the swastika was a symbol of life and good fortune before Hitler adopted it as the emblem for the Nazi party. Today, the swastika is to most people a symbol of hatred and evil.

September 1, 1939
Germany invades Poland.
World War II begins.

September 10, 1939
Canada declares
war on Germany.

May 10, 1940
Germany invades France
Holland and Belgium.

**Britain and France
declare war on Germany.**
September 3, 1939

**Germany invades
Denmark and Norway.**
April 9, 1940

Holland surrenders.
May 15, 1940

In the spring, German troops advanced north and westward. By mid-1940, Norway, Denmark, Belgium, France, and the Netherlands had fallen to Hitler's war machine as it hammered its way across Europe.

In the early hours of May 10, 1940, sleeping Dutch citizens woke to the roar of low-flying airplanes and stared in disbelief as hundreds of soldiers parachuted from the skies. Hitler's troops were invading Holland. The Kingdom of the Netherlands was under attack. Turning on their **radios**, the Dutch people listened to a special broadcast instructing them to cover their windows with tape so the glass would not shatter when the bombs came.

And the bombs did come.

Major airfields and the city of Rotterdam were reduced to rubble. When the Nazis threatened to destroy other cities, Holland surrendered. The Dutch people began living the nightmare that would last for the next five years.

Out of Harm's Way

Within days of Hitler's invasion, Queen Wilhelmina, ruler of the Netherlands, escaped to England with her ministers and the Dutch Royal Family to avoid capture. She tried to keep up the spirits of her people through radio broadcasts.

However, under the constant menace of German air attacks, even England was not safe. The Queen's daughter and heir to the throne, Princess Juliana, and the royal granddaughters had to find shelter in a safer country, somewhere much farther away. They chose Canada, a partner in the Commonwealth.

Princess Juliana And Children Reach Halifax

Heiress Apparent To Netherlands Throne Coming to Ottawa

By JOHN LEBLANC.
Canadian Press Staff Writer.

HALIFAX, June 11. — A Dutch naval squadron today brought Princess Juliana and her two infant children to Canadian haven.

The Ottawa Journal, June 11, 1940
Courtesy of the City of Ottawa Archives

June 11, 1940
Princess Juliana arrives in Canada with her daughters Beatrix and Irene.

January 19, 1943
Princess Margriet is born in Ottawa's Civic Hospital.

June 6, 1944
Allied troops storm the beaches of Normandy, France.

Japan bombs Pearl Harbor. The United States enter the war.
December 7, 1941

Princess Margriet is baptized in Ottawa's St. Andrews Church.
June 29, 1943

Canadian troops fight to liberate Holland.
Sept. 44 – April 45

While her husband, Prince Bernhard, stayed in London at the Queen's side, Crown Princess Juliana and her children, nine-month-old baby Irene and two-and-a-half-year-old Beatrix, sailed for Canada on the Dutch cruiser Sumatra. They entered Halifax harbour on June 11, 1940, where they were welcomed by a small group of Dutch and Canadian officials before continuing on their journey to Canada's capital, Ottawa.

Shortly after their arrival in Ottawa, the family moved into their wartime home at 120 Lansdowne Road. Occasionally, Prince Bernhard would visit when he travelled to Canada on military business. In winter, Beatrix and Irene filled their days by building snow forts and ice skating. They learned to swim and ride their bikes in summer. Later, when they were old enough, the children attended nursery school and Rockcliffe Park Public School.

Princess Juliana showed her support of the Canadian war effort by joining the everyday activities of the women around her. She knitted scarves and sweaters for Canadian soldiers, volunteered at a second-hand shop, and donated her blood for the Red Cross. ❦

Princess learning to swim

From left: Queen Wilhelmina and Princesses Irene, Beatrix and Juliana

Rockcliffe Park Public School

Photos courtesy of the City of Ottawa Archives

Instant History Facts

🌷 During the war, Canadian women sewed quilts and clothing and knitted mittens, scarves, socks and sweaters for soldiers overseas. They gave blood and rolled bandages for the Red Cross. They prepared small packages for sailors, known as ditty-bags, which held small comforts of home, including tooth powder, shaving soap, cigarettes and writing paper. They raised money by selling war stamps and certificates.

With so many men fighting overseas, Canadian women filled positions on assembly lines, making everything from parachutes to torpedoes. They also worked as butchers, bakers, riveters, welders, mechanics, bus and streetcar drivers. Nearly 50 000 served in the armed forces at home and abroad as nurses, teachers in training centres, cooks in mess halls, pilots ferrying service aircraft between squadrons and air storage units, and as drivers of ambulances, jeeps and other light vehicles. More than 3 000 women worked dangerously close to enemy lines.

🌷 Children also helped. They joined knitting clubs and put on talent shows to raise funds for the Junior Red Cross. They collected newspapers and other paper products to be recycled as gas mask canisters and hand grenade containers and to wrap supplies that were shipped to Allied troops overseas. They collected metal objects, including their own lead soldiers, that were melted down and used for war munitions.

"SHELL OUT, SHELL OUT"

"Shell out, shell out!" This is the cry of the three young paper salvagers in the picture above. The Boy Scouts of Canada are giving their time in various war drives, not the least of these being the collection of waste paper. They realize that paper is a war material, essential both to the armed forces and to war production. Paper is used in camouflage strips and netting and parachutes . . . gas mask cannisters and hand grenade containers are made of paper, and some 700,000 different items are paper-wrapped and boxed and shipped from North America to the United Nations' armies.

*Courtesy of the Westmount Examiner,
February 18, 1944*

Hope is Born

In the spring of 1942, Princess Juliana had happy news: she was going to have a baby! In anticipation, delighted nurses at Ottawa's Civic Hospital sewed bedding and prepared a small bassinet.

However, one problem did arise. Since this new prince or princess could one day become the ruler of the Netherlands, many considered it necessary that the baby be Dutch-born. But clearly Princess Juliana could not travel back to Holland. Fortunately, a solution was found. Before the baby was born, the Canadian Government prepared a document declaring the place of birth as *extraterritorial* – or outside of Canadian territory – which meant that the baby would be born a Dutch citizen, though in a foreign country.

The birth of Princess Margriet Francisca of the Netherlands on January 19, 1943, brought new hope to the people of the Netherlands. 🌷

*Christening of
Princess Margriet*

Princess Juliana Is Well But Prince Bernhard Nervous

Princess Beatrix, Four, Wonders if New Baby Will Resemble Any of Her Dolls

Princess Juliana spent a quiet, restful night at the Ottawa Civic Hospital, where she is expecting the birth of her third child, and her condition today was again described as "excellent and normal".

The development today was that the little Princesses Beatrix and Irene, somewhat alarmed by the absence of their mother, had been informed that she had gone to the North to fetch a baby brother or a baby sister for them. Their mother would be back in a few days, they were told.

*The Ottawa Journal, January 18, 1943
Courtesy of the City of Ottawa Archives*

*Princess Juliana
with baby Margriet*

*Photos courtesy of the
City of Ottawa Archives*

Instant History Facts

🌷 Princess Margriet is named after the *marguerite* (meaning daisy), a flower identified by her grandmother as a symbol of hope and resistance to the Nazis.

And they needed reason to hope.

Back in the Netherlands, each day had become a fight for survival. The Nazis stole much of the food, warm clothes, and other supplies for themselves. They gave ration coupons to the Dutch people to exchange for meals or groceries, but often there was not enough food. Meals consisted of little more than bread, potatoes, and sugar beets. In entire neighbourhoods and villages, men between the ages of 17 and 40 were often rounded up to be used as slave labour in German factories, leaving women and children to scrounge for things to eat and pieces of coal to heat themselves with. A curfew was also established and anyone caught outdoors after sundown could be shot on sight.

Gestapo eat lunch while Dutch people wait for leftovers

Courtesy of the National Archives of Canada

Ration coupons consisted of small stamp-like rectangles that had to be cut out of the sheet and handed over to the shopkeeper. These ration coupons were for butter (boter), potatoes (aardappelen), and for any food "in general" (algemeen) that was temporarily available.

Courtesy of the Atlas Van Stolk collection

Despite all of this, the Dutch people fought back. When the Nazis ordered them to give up their antiques, jewellery, and other metal treasures to be melted down for ammunition, the Dutch buried what they could in their gardens for safekeeping. Jews were now forced to live in enclosed areas called ghettos and wear a yellow Star of David for identification. When the Nazis began taking them away, many were hidden in homes of friends and strangers for months and even years. However, this did not prevent the deportation of over 100 000 Dutch Jews to Nazi death camps.

Bit by bit, a secret network of people called the Dutch Resistance was formed to fight against their enemy. When the Nazis took over the newspapers, the Resistance printed and distributed posters and pamphlets to keep the people informed about the war. Resistance fighters were also involved in sabotage and spying: they blew up bridges, destroyed railroads, and coded and decoded secret messages from Britain—all to create obstacles for Hitler's army. The Resistance also forged identification papers and ration coupons to help the people to survive. Resistance fighters who were caught were tortured and often killed.

Anne Frank and her family lived in Amsterdam

Courtesy of
Yad Vashem,
Jerusalem

*Star of David
Jood means Jew
in Dutch*

Courtesy of the
Montreal Holocaust
Memorial Centre

A forbidden radio was the only luxury retained in this home where everything burnable had been stripped for fuel. Amsterdam, 1944-1945

Courtesy of the
National Archives
of Canada

So Many Lives Lost

On June 6, 1944, known as D-Day, 156 000 British, Canadian, and American troops landed on the beaches of Normandy, France. This marked the beginning of the final phase of the war in Europe.

In July and August the **Allies** fought westward into France, liberating the cities of Rouen, Dieppe, Boulogne, and Calais. They moved quickly and soon reached Belgium. But by then the routes that brought food and equipment to the soldiers stretched all the way back to Normandy. A quicker way to transport supplies to the troops needed to be found. A seaport closer to the frontlines was the answer.

In Belgium, the city of Antwerp had a port, but it was almost 80 kilometres inland. To reach the sea, ships had to make their way through the Scheldt Estuary, a winding river with waters peppered with mines and shores well-defended by the Germans. The First Canadian Army was given the task of clearing the banks of the Scheldt.

Instant History Facts

We call "**Allies**" the group of nations that joined together to fight the Nazis. Canada, England, France and the United States were part of this group.

It is estimated that 10 000 Allied soldiers were wounded, killed or went missing in action on **D-Day**. Prior to D-Day, Canadians had attempted to storm the beaches at the French port of Dieppe on August 19, 1942. On that day, which became one of the darkest days of the Second World War for Canadian troops, 3 367 of a total of 4 960 Canadian soldiers from the Second Canadian Division, were killed, wounded or captured.

Canadian troops in the First and Second World Wars fought under the Canadian **Red Ensign**. Many versions of this flag, inspired by the ensigns of the British Merchant Marine, were flown from 1870 until the red maple leaf flag was declared the National Flag of Canada on February 15, 1965.

View from LCI(L) 306 of the 2nd Canadian (262nd RN) Flotilla showing ships of Force 'J' en route to France on **D-Day**

Courtesy of the National Archives of Canada

The **Red Ensign**

The Battle of the Scheldt

*The army commander, **General Crerar**, sits with St. Nicholas at a party at the Canadian army mess in Tilburg* 🌷

Beginning in mid-September to early November, 1944, the Canadians fought bitterly against the German army, at times waist-deep in muddy waters along the banks of the Scheldt. As the 2nd and 4th Canadian Divisions cleared the east and north shores, the 3rd Division cleared the south. When the battle for the Scheldt was over, more than 6 000 Canadian soldiers lay dead or wounded. The port of Antwerp was now open and the southern part of Holland was liberated.

During the months of December and January, Canadian troops rested and planned for their next battle, for more fighting was to come. Many soldiers were welcomed into the homes of Dutch families, where warm ties of friendship were made and would not be forgotten.

Instant History Facts

🌷 The First Canadian Army, under the leadership of **General Harry Crerar**, included five Canadian Divisions, as well as soldiers from the United States and Europe.

🌷 In September 1944, believing that Holland would soon be free, the Dutch government sent coded radio messages from London instructing the Dutch Resistance to organize a country-wide railway strike to interrupt German military transports. On the designated morning, not one of the many thousands of railway workers showed up for work, bringing all transportation to a standstill. To punish the Dutch, the Nazis cut off all their food supplies, leaving an already starving population without nourishment at the approach of winter.

🌷 Soldiers made toys to be handed out as presents to the children and organized parties to celebrate the Feast of St. Nicholas, on December 6th. On the Eve of the Feast of St. Nicholas, Dutch children leave their shoes out in the hopes of finding them filled with candies and small presents in the morning.

Canadian soldiers made toys to be handed out as Christmas presents 🌷

Photos courtesy of the National Archives of Canada

The Battle of the Rhineland

By February, one German stronghold remained – the Rhineland. This was where most of Germany's war industries were located. On February 8, 1945, the First Canadian Army advanced into Germany west of the Rhine River, pushing the enemy back and clearing a passageway along the left bank of the river for Allied troops to cross over. Fighting conditions were as difficult if not worse than those of the Scheldt. Unusually mild temperatures and heavy rains turned the frozen battle ground into fields of oozing mud. As Canadian soldiers once again waded waist-deep across flooded lands, more than 5 000 were killed or wounded.

By the end of the month-long battle of the Rhineland, the Allies had broken through Hitler's last line of defense.

In mid-March, the First Canadian Army began to liberate the parts of Holland that were still occupied by the Nazis. While the 2nd, 3rd, and 4th Canadian Divisions cleared the northern part of Holland, the 1st and 5th Canadian Divisions cleared the central and western parts.

By then, the food and fuel shortages had taken their toll on the Dutch population. With no gas or electricity, people had cut up trees, advertising signs and park benches, and stripped their homes and bombed out buildings of staircases, furniture, books and any other materials they could burn for warmth. For food, many ate tulip bulbs. As the Canadians entered one town after another, they were welcomed by cheering Dutch people who wept for joy at the sight of their liberators. ♆

Youth removing teak-wood blocks between streetcar tracks during the fuel shortage. Amsterdam, 1944-1945

Photos courtesy of the National Archives of Canada

Instant History Facts

♆ Over 16 000 Dutch men, women and children died of cold and hunger during the "Hunger Winter" months of 1944-1945.

Boy outside black market restaurant hoping for food handout. Children often carried spoons to grasp any opportunity. Amsterdam, 1944-1945

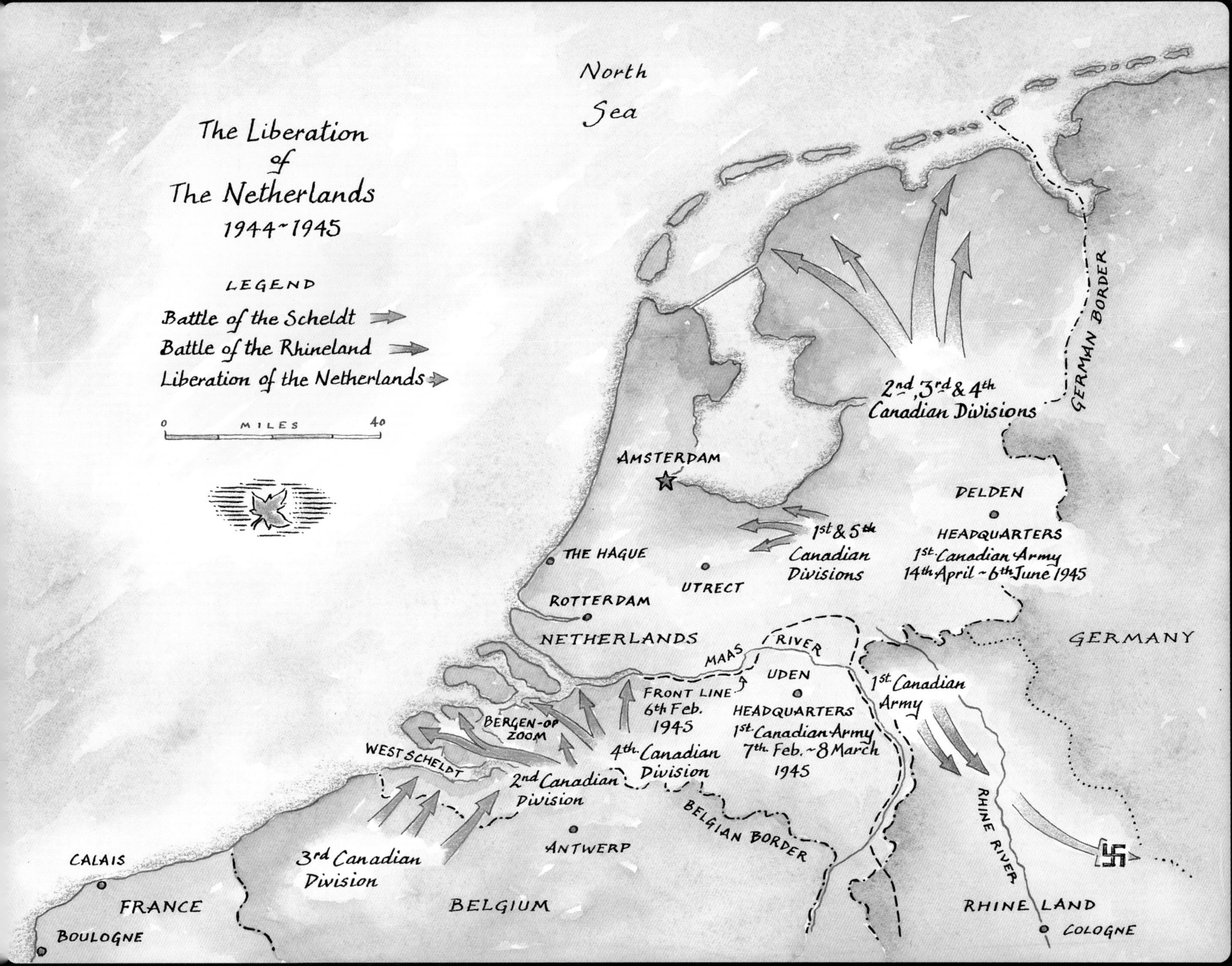

North
Sea

The Liberation
of
The Netherlands
1944~1945

LEGEND

Battle of the Scheldt →
Battle of the Rhineland →
Liberation of the Netherlands →

0 — MILES — 40

GERMAN BORDER

2nd, 3rd & 4th
Canadian Divisions

AMSTERDAM ☆

1st & 5th
Canadian
Divisions

DELDEN ●

HEADQUARTERS
1st Canadian Army
14th April ~ 6th June 1945

THE HAGUE ●

UTRECT ●

ROTTERDAM ●

NETHERLANDS

MAAS RIVER

UDEN ●

1st Canadian
Army

GERMANY

FRONT LINE
6th Feb.
1945

HEADQUARTERS
1st Canadian Army
7th Feb. ~ 8 March
1945

BERGEN-OP-
ZOOM

4th Canadian
Division

WEST SCHELDT

2nd Canadian
Division

BELGIAN BORDER

RHINE RIVER

3rd Canadian
Division

ANTWERP ●

CALAIS ●

FRANCE

BELGIUM

RHINE LAND

COLOGNE ●

BOULOGNE ●

Freedom

In the spring of 1945 it was clear that the war would soon be over. Most of Holland was now liberated, with the exception of the West. To rescue the five million starving Dutch citizens who remained under Nazi rule, a truce was negotiated with the Germans to allow food drops. From April 29 to May 8, with the help of the Royal Canadian Air Force (RCAF) 405 Squadron marking the delivery drop zones, British and American bomber planes dropped over 12 000 tons of food and supplies into Holland. Grateful, the Dutch spelled out thank-you messages on the ground with flowers and bedsheets for the pilots to see.

The war did not resume after the cease-fire. On May 5, 1945, Canadian Lieutenant-General Charles Foulkes accepted the surrender of all German troops in Holland.

On May 8, 1945, the war in Europe was over.

Allied Forces food drop over Schiphol Airport. Amsterdam area, May 2, 1945

Courtesy of the National Archives of Canada

The Gazette.

MONTREAL, TUESDAY, MAY 8, 1945.—THIRTY-SIX PAGES

PRICE FIVE CENTS

GERMANY SURRENDERS
WAR IN EUROPE ENDS EXCEPT FOR CZECHOSLOVAK POCKET

Courtesy of the Montreal Gazette

Instant History Facts

Frank V. Stanton of Hamilton, Ontario, participated in "Operation Manna," the code name for the British Royal Air Force mission to air drop food supplies into Holland (the United-States lead a similar mission called "Operation Chowhound"). Planes flew so low to the ground – to avoid damage to the food – that Frank recalled waving from the air to a Dutch citizen in a windmill, and that person waving back to him. Pilots and flight crew members also contributed to the drops by making tiny parachutes out of handkerchiefs and attaching their cookie and chocolate rations for the Dutch children.

May 5, 1945
Germans in Holland surrender.

The war in Europe ends.
May 8, 1945

August, 1945
Princess Margriet steps onto liberated Dutch soil for the first time.

The first Tulip Festival is held in Ottawa.
Spring, 1953

May, 1995
The 50th anniversary of the liberation of Holland.

The 50th anniversary of the Canadian Tulip Festival.
May, 2002

Vehicles driven by soldiers of the 1st Canadian Corps were swamped with civilians when the troops liberated Utrecht on May 7, 1945.

Courtesy of the National Archives of Canada

When the Dutch Royal Family returned to their homeland, not only did they find Dutch citizens picking up the pieces of their shattered lives, they also discovered a people deeply thankful to the Canadians who played a vital role in their freedom.

Instant History Facts

During the spring and summer months that followed the end of the war in Europe, many Canadian soldiers helped Dutch citizens rebuild their houses, bridges, and dykes while awaiting their return home. During these months, many friendships were formed between young Dutch women and Canadian soldiers. When the soldiers returned home, more than 1 800 war brides and 400 children came to Canada with them.

Lente 1945
Ondergang van het „1000-jarig rijk"....smeet

DE ZEELANDSCHE,
GE ZIET HET KLAAR,
ONTVANGT DE GEALLIEERDEN
MET MILD GEBAAR.

Vintage Dutch postcards commemorating the end of the war.

Courtesy of the Atlas Van Stolk collections.

In 1945, shortly after her return to Holland, Princess Juliana presented Canada with 100 000 tulip bulbs in recognition of the role the country played during the grim years of the Second World War. Each year since, Canada has received a gift of 20 000 tulip bulbs, which are planted in and around the capital of Ottawa in the fall so that they may bloom come spring.

Malak Karsh, one of Canada's greatest photographers, was the driving force behind the creation of Ottawa's Canadian Tulip Festival. Malak took great pleasure in capturing the beauty of Canada's landscapes on film and was particularly fond of the tulips that bloomed every spring on Parliament Hill. Following his suggestion to the city's Board of Trade to have an annual event in celebration of the flowers, Ottawa held its first official tulip festival in 1953.

Instant History Facts

Malak Karsh's 1963 photograph, entitled "Paper and Politics," depicting logs floating on the Ottawa River below Parliament Hill, was reproduced over 4 billion times on the back of the former Canadian one-dollar bill. In 1987, the Canadian one-dollar bill was replaced with the eleven-sided $1 coin, depicting the loon, which we now call "the loonie."

One-dollar bill

©Bank of Canada - used and altered with permission

Malak Karsh - Parliament Buildings With Tulips

Malak Karsh - Canadian Tulip Festival - National Gallery of Canada
Photos courtesy of Barbara Karsh

Malak with "Malak Karsh" Triumph Tulips
Credit: Photographed by Barbara Karsh

A Lasting Friendship

Commemorative stamps

Over the years, and to this day, the ties of friendship between Canada and the Netherlands are still witnessed on both sides of the Atlantic Ocean.

In 1995, the 50th anniversary of the liberation drew thousands of Canadian war veterans back to Holland, where once again they were welcomed into the homes of Dutch families. During the two-week festivities, many retired soldiers revisited the people, the cities and villages, and the battlegrounds they had come to know so long ago.

Private Thomas Delaney

In 2002, Princess Margriet made one of her return visits to Canada for the 50th Anniversary of the tulip festival. She attended a number of events, one of which was the christening of a special variety of tulip called "The Canadian Liberator."

The Dutch people have also ensured that future generations will not forget Canada's sacrifice or the devastation of war. At nightfall on Christmas Eve at the Canadian War Cemetery in Holten, schoolchildren light candles and place them on each of the more than 1 300 graves. And on May 4th, the date on which the Dutch remember those who died during Word War II, they recite poems and decorate the graves with flowers. The children do this as gestures of appreciation and to remind themselves of how very fortunate they are to live in a country that is not at war.

Instant History Facts

On the morning of April 8, 1945, nineteen-year-old Thomas Delaney from Beauharnois, Quebec, was shot in the hip by a German soldier. Private Delaney was recovered and brought to a barn where Dutch adults and children were hiding. When he returned to Holland in 1995 he was able to find the barn where he had been hidden and also met up with one of the children, now a grown woman, who remembered the event in detail.

In 2002, on the occasion of the 50th anniversary of the Canadian Tulip Festival, Canada Post issued a series of commemorative stamps and plates featuring the colourful spring flower.

Of the 7 600 Canadians who died liberating the Netherlands, more than 4 500 are buried in the Canadian War Cemeteries in Holten, Groesbeek and Bergen Op Zoom.

The Canadian Tulip Festival, the largest in the world, is celebrated every year in Ottawa. Visitors come from around the globe to see more than three million tulips paint a kaleidoscope of colour on the Capital's grounds. The beauty of the floral gift that began in 1945 is a reminder of the safe haven we provided so long ago and a tribute to the thousands of Canadians who fought and died during the dreadful months of conflict that gave way to the liberation of Holland.

So now when you see a tulip, remember and honour those who wrote this part of our history.

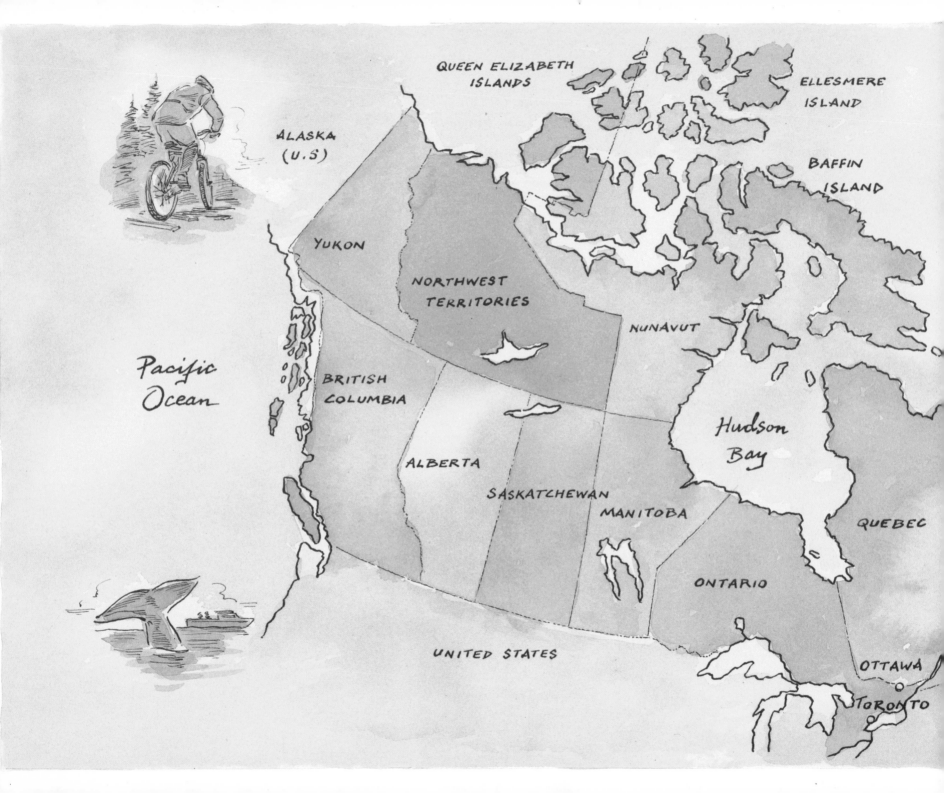